# THE WELL IN THE RAIN

Other books by the author:

POETRY
The Shifting of Stones
Behind the Green Curtain
This Far North
Three Songs of Home
The Book of Winter Cures
What Darkness Covers

EDITED
*As the Poet Said...*

PLAYS
*On Famine Road*
with Paul Goetzee and Jack Bradley
*The Third Policeman* by Flann O'Brien
adapted with Jack Bradley

# Tony Curtis

*The Well in the Rain*

NEW AND SELECTED POEMS

*For Sheila,*

*Warm wishes,*

*Tony*

*19 - X - 06*

*Gu. (7 ZoR)*

**Arc**
PUBLICATIONS

2006

Published by Arc Publications
Nanholme Mill, Shaw Wood Road
Todmorden OL14 6DA, UK

Printed by Biddles Ltd
King's Lynn, Norfolk, UK

ISBN-13: 978 1904614 27 2
ISBN-10: 1 904614 27 2

### ACKNOWLEDGEMENTS

As well as previously uncollected poems, *The Well in the Rain* includes work from the following collections: *The Shifting of Stones* (Beaver Row Press, 1986), *Behind the Green Curtain* (Beaver Row Press, 1988), *This Far North* (Dedalus Press, 1993), *Three Songs of Home* (Dedalus Press, 1996), *The Book of Winter Cures* (Black Hills Press 2002), *What Darkness Covers* (Arc Publications, 2003).

*Crossings: 21 Bridges* was published in a limited edition by The Design Factory in 2005. A shorter version of the poem is published here as *Seventeen Bridges*.

*Seven Haiku for Sahoko's Drawing* was written in response to Sahoko Blake's drawing 'Moon' for Poetry Ireland's 'Rhyme & Resin' exhibition and auction 2005.

*The Knot, Odd, Anniversary* & *The Poet and the Mouse* were first published in the Clifden Anthology.

*Odd, Dublin, Beckettian Clerihews* & *The Poet and the Mouse* were first broadcast on RTÉ Radio 1.

The author would like to thank Mary and Oisín, Theo Dorgan, Paula Meehan, Pat Mooney and everyone at Arc Publications for all their help in putting this book together.

Cover Design & Photography: Pat Mooney
© Pat Mooney, 2006

The Publishers acknowledge financial
assistance from ACE Yorkshire

**Editor for UK / Ireland: Jo Shapcott**

*Perhaps my best years are gone...*
*But I wouldn't want them back.*
*Not with the fire in me now.*
**Samuel Beckett**

*For my father*
*Kevin Curtis (1921-2004)*
*gone with the autumn leaves*

# Contents

*from* THREE SONGS OF HOME (1998)

*from* WHAT DARKNESS COVERS (2003)

NEW POEMS: TOSSING THE FEATHERS (2006)

*From* The Shifting of Stones
(1986)

# Home Thoughts

I was born in Dublin
between the docklands
and the Hill of Howth.
A Catholic's youth,
said prayers beside the quiet
altar of my little bed.
A Catholic's education,
the soft swish of leather
against the dark robes.

The clock ticking slowly
through classes in Irish and English;
I learnt the poetry of fear.
Lived for the summer months,
the holy days: Easter; Whit;
'Hail glorious Saint Patrick'.
Awaited the death of de Valera.
Through those school-days the taste
of freedom was always on my mind.

I remember the joy of being
called early from class to sing
soprano in the school choir.
Bored, I stood at the bottom
of a small squad of boys
gazing out as the clouds pushed past
towards Wexford, Galway, Donegal,
or perhaps, like the mail boat
I took, towards Holyhead.

Land of dead Kings and old Queens.
Land of Shakespeare, who saw through both
and reached into our soul.
Land of mad Cromwell, blind Milton.
Land of that epic idiot Spenser.
Did you know there's a Curtis in
'The Taming of the Shrew'?
An aged servant who dreams of better times,
and spends his days opening doors for others.
So many of the Irish in London,
myself included, unrehearsed,
could have played his role so well.

Seven years I spent in England.
I didn't then, nor do I now,
understand why I left these shores.
Though when I stand on a bog on such
an unholy day as this, knowing that every
wet shadow I meet along the road
is heading for shelter,
it's only natural to think
that in my day Dublin was much like this –
a wilderness for childhood. In my youth
the world and its streets were cold.
That's my story.

# The Shifting of Stones

Old shipyards
like old women
wither and die;
too much water
in their bones.

Yet, when they
were young, their
still, quiet waters
offered safe harbour;
homes for weary bones.

The song and dance
of a salty sailor charmed
my mother. The sea rocked
against her sides,
calm until the storms.

Now the stones
have shifted,
the gantries rusted.
The blessing of ships
has not been heard for years.

# The Morning After Eden

I was born old,
conjured out
of a cracked rib.

Your cold hands
bent me into this
peculiar shape.

I screamed
with pain.
I hated you.

Day after day,
your cold eyes
stared at my nakedness.

I ate your fucking apple,
ate until I was sick
and you dragged me away

by the hair.
Your parched laughter
has made you hoarse.

My body is sore
from your weight.
You have not bathed

since you were dirt.
Sleep can't take you away,
you are part of me.

# The Suitcase

This is the Kilburn High Road
running up towards Cricklewood
away from England's Edgeware Road
where the homeless Irish come
each with his father's battered suitcase,
though their father may have never left home.
They used to buy them at the summer fairs
for that day when their time would come,
or get them off a friend who died,
his lifelong journey finally done.
That's how my father stayed in his fields.
His suitcase travelled to him
from an Irish woman with a soft Kerry voice,
whose children's eyes were Irish blue
and accents East End Cockney.
She had married three times in England
and returned sadly widowed again.
The locals said "she deserved what she got
the saintless, ungodly woman."
Yet they listened discreetly to the stories she told
of how one husband left in a blitz of booze,
another in a blitz of bombs,
the last one dying on a beach outside Calais
his toes barely touching French soil.
She used to giggle at the thought,
said it reminded her of once
when he danced on Brighton beach
in nothing but his cotton drawers.
When she died the priest brought round her suitcase.
My father left it by the door.
In our kitchen someone was always leaving home.

# The Disturbance

A bomb shatters the silence of George Street,
sending clouds of dust down chimneys.
In seconds the dull thud dies away,
only a milk bottle rolling over the pavement
disturbs the silence with its circular sound.
Unshaven men in pyjamas stand like convicts
framed in the doorways of their cells,
or lean out windows like old farmers
on wooden gates, staring over concrete fields
whose walls hold nothing in.
Women half dressed, still warm from sleep,
hold children's hands and let tired faces hang
like flowers withering after daylight or water;
behind them kettles whistle
and toast burns under the grill.
Along another quiet road
a man, pedalling an old bicycle,
whistles a familiar Irish air
as he creaks up a hill towards home,
the morning paper in his pocket,
secure, folded like a job well done.

# Cold as the Irish Sea

*Ní bheidh ár leithéidí arís ann.*
                    T. Ó Criomthain
                    *An tOileánach*


Begin again with no ideas,
with death or prayer,
with a dream image
of a man behind a spade
like a priest behind a cross,
his hands wrapped around
the wooden handle, his eyes
digging through his thoughts.

A man stripped to the waist,
tired as the leather in his shoes
or the cragged hills
that creep away from him for miles
towards the black mountains
he has never been beyond.
"What's out there?" he sometimes
mumbles to himself,
but never quite catches
what the voice is saying.
Here, this day and tomorrow
are always the same.

So should I begin
with the rain coming down
like a bow across
the strings of a fiddle,
or a voice in a doorway

coming in, saying "wind's coming up"
while his coat's coming off,
leaving the door ajar.
His forgetfulness reveals
an old bicycle
leaning against a wall,
quietly rusting to the music
that the rain makes
dancing on the saddle.

But as a child
when I walked these lanes
visions would appear.
Streams became oceans
where, with bulging eyes,
I would watch my mother's
famine frail hands
launch withered leaves
upon the treacherous waters.
They were the hunger ships
that stole my people
from this land.

West, who would conceive
that such a little word
could, like a pass-word
whispered in darkness,
or light pouring
in through a keyhole,
spill a glimpse of freedom
into so many tired

and wasted lives.
I have seen them
lift up their ragged bodies
as if fed upon a whisper,
walking West.

But what's three thousand miles
to a soul who has never been
beyond his own front yard,
merely a corridor into darkness,
a strange place to die.

I was eighty-two last birthday,
but I did not celebrate.
No, I merely stood by the door
and through these blind eyes
stared out down the valley.
I have no memory of what I saw,
but if I was to look out now
all would be as it was on that day,
unless the leaves have fallen.
No, this is the summer time.
I have felt the heat upon my face
and know, if you were to look out now
over the fields you would see him,
old Mather's son, mumbling to the land
like his father and his father's father.
God, you could die here and never leave.
A thousand churches with their moats
of ivied headstones, testify to the rebirth
of the Murphy's, Malley's and O'Dwyer's.

# Gilhaney's Nightmare

*after* Flann O'Brien


Now back to bicycles.
I have spent two weeks
getting to know the inside of them.
They are hollow and dark.

I went in through the lamp.
Hello! My voice echoed
through a musty corridor. I reached
behind and brought the lamp with me.

Just below the handle-bars
I pushed open a great oak door.
It revealed a country lane
running off into the distance.

It collapsed from exhaustion
at the top of a hill
and rolled all the way back to me.
I think it died, because

suddenly the lights went out
and a hand grabbed my shoulder
pulling me back through the oak door.
I swung around shining the lamp.

The corridor seemed dark and empty
as before. Only a stout black constable's bike
that earlier had gone unnoticed,
leaned suspiciously against the dark.

In other words, it stood there by itself.
An invisible policeman, I thought.
I waited for the cough.
Sure enough, it came.

I dropped the lamp,
hurled myself down the corridor
and leapt out of the bicycle
the way I had come.

I had no idea where I'd been
but I am sure it wasn't Ireland.

*from* Behind the Green Curtain
(1988)

# The Touch

I

The West of Ireland is an empty church
built of curdled blood and brittle bone,
of sheep's placenta, flies, hedge and scutch.
Blessed are those who cross its graveyard of stone.
A while ago I saw the priest, a man of thirty
or forty, ambling across the back of the bog.
On a mission from God? No, he passed me
wearing a walkman, he was simply out walking his dog.
And I though ot my temptation on the Bog of Allen
that day with Mary Molloy from outside Enniscorthy,
when no priest passed or came near the ditch.
As we stood naked, the last of our clothes fallen,
I heard a voice say "bogs never saw the like in Galway."
Surely, in all the world, that Eden had God's touch.

II

Shortly after I finished that poem
a farmer wandered into the back bar
of the Milestone and told me he was on to me.
He had seen me standing at his gate
with my pen and bits of paper,
noting his crops, counting his sheep,
his cows, his fields. Leering at his wife.

"You, you're a land inspector. A whore
that lives on other men's misfortune."

"I'm not," says I, "I'm the bad end of a poet."

"God forgive you," says he, "a poet is it,
you and your kind have been a plague
on our country since blind Raftery
and Ó Bruadair took to the road
with their curses and their curious thoughts.
Damn you and your dirty books,
and your blind eyes that have never
seen the light inside a church."

I never met that man before,
nor have I seen him since,
though often I have felt his coldness
move over my grave, his spittle
run slowly down my headstone.

# Rowing to the Island

It began with a blade of grass,
the end of the road, the field
down to the rocks where the boats
left for the island. Oars dipped,
water fled, the boat moved out.
The oarsman sang of Michael O'Dwyer
drowned off the isle of Inis na Bró
so long ago only his song and a stone
in the cemetery at Dunquin recall him.

I had come to see the white strand,
the fields and lanes of the Blaskets.
I wanted to stand among the ruins
of Ó Criomthain's house and stare his
chiselled stare back at the dark island
of Ireland. A wave lifted, the oarsman
bent his back, his strong arms tensed:
"I'm forgetting the words to that song."

Then he asked if I knew that no one
was ever buried on the island except
for those who came into the world without
a beating heart, those baptised by their
mother with rain water or sea water.
"They were laid to sleep in the earth
among the ruins of an ancient church.
The islanders feared the dead's stare
more than they feared the sea's rage.

Until the dead were coffined on the island
women would not move outside their doors.

Even tall young men passed by in twos.
The island itself is dead now, uninhabited,
but I've no doubt its stones are haunted.
Often, on summer days, when I sit in the
cavity of my father's cottage I can feel
his presence. He is sitting in the corner,
his old eyes are looking out to sea, he is
waiting for the last boat to come home.

Man and boy I've known these islands,
the lost lanes across their backs,
but like my father and my father's father
this sack of salted bones will be shoved
into the earth at the church in Dunquin."
A wave lifted; again the oarsman bent his back,
his strong arms tensed. The oars dipped,
the water fled, the boat moved on.

# Behind the Green Curtain

That winter she froze
behind the green curtain.

Cold rose through her toes
into her bones. Her hair grew.

His hands caught her form.
His eyes the shadows on her skin.

Damp days folded one into another
until he coughed thin blood,

walked towards the light and heaved
up the great Georgian window,

taped shut for years against
the artist's fear of dust on oil.

Forgetting her nakedness she went
to take him from the open window.

He jumped. Blew his life out
as easily as he would a candle.

She leaned out, it was a red painting
he'd made with his life and broken bones.

A shopkeeper's eyes moved over
the white curves of her breasts.

Did he think them quarrelling lovers?
Did he imagine a scented room,

tossed sheets on a tossed bed,
two white pillows,

clothes left where they had fallen,
a skirt covering a chair's modesty?

She walked slowly back across
the painter's room. Then wrapped

the green curtain over her bare shoulders,
feeling warm for the first time in days.

# Homage

*for* Samuel Beckett


My brother is a committed man.
He entered Portrane Lunatic Asylum
on the of June this year,
the year of our Lord as they say.
He owns them all you know.
Every day of every week,
every hour of every day,
every minute of ever hour,
down to the last second
of recorded time and beyond it.

I knew a man once who
took it into his head
to believe none of it.
He died an atrocious death,
calling for a priest.
I heard this from my aunt
and she should know,
she was the one who wouldn't go;
merely stood by the bedroom door
wagging her gnarled, nicotined finger,
the one with the broken nail,
saying: "I told you so.
I told you so. I told you so."

I cycle out to see the brother
every Friday. Crossing Feltrim
I always think of you, on that
spring morning, stretched out

in the long grass with Winnie.
Your first love and last, you said.
Though I seem to recall
you mentioning somewhere
a day on the river
in a boat among the reeds.
So long ago. Rust round the rim
of the memory. Cobwebs to the core.

The ruin on the hill is gone.
Did you know it was a windmill?
I found that out a month ago
in a coffee table book
someone has written about you.
A few hundred photographs
that charge through your life
into the valley of death.
From where you now sit
you must be able to see it all
clear as a spring day.

Imagine, if you had not lived
I'd never have known the ruin
was a mill or thought of you
stretched out on the hill
each time I pass this way.
If I had not been born
it wouldn't have affected
your life in the least.
Though you would have sold
fewer books. Thirteen to be exact.

# Siren off Inisheer

A Japanese kimono seemed out of place
in the draughty three roomed cottage
sunk into the back of Inisheer, but
there you were, breasts tucked like
oranges in the colourful soft silk.

You arched your back and a shy ghost
lifted the kimono off your shoulders,
it slid to the floor and you were gone.
Through the small cruciform window
I shivered as you plunged and surfaced

like a seal a few yards beyond the rocks.
Then I noticed the caps rising on the pier.
The eyes of the three women by the front wall.
I could hear your siren's call from the sea.
I lifted your kimono and the latch off the door.

# A Winter's Tale

The road led up off over the mountains,
stopping at the village with a pond
that no one ever painted, but was like
those you see in landscape paintings.

They stopped the car. Ordered two pints.
Thick cream flowed from the heads down
onto the wooden counter. They drank.
Buttoned their coats when leaving.

The smell of beer was on their breath
when they pushed through the half-door,
upsetting a child's tricycle. Plates
splintered as the woman hit the floor.

They left by the back door. Taking shirts
off the line to wipe the blood from their hands.

# On a Mountain Road

*for* Oisín

The first fall of snow has frozen
the earth white as a dead man's hand.
From where I stand on this lonely bog
they call the feather bed, to the
curve in the road, between the grotto
and the graveyard, at quiet Glencree,
the sky is gone. So too the mountains
with their patchwork of hawthorns
that quilts the land into fields.
Rivers remain. Somewhere salmon leap
to catch the white flies before they
melt on the river's wet back. Sheep die.

I have brought my small son out
to creature this white wilderness
with the memory of our footprints,
the dark shadow that we cast.
His small hand steadies my step.
His eyes, slit like a hawk's, scan.
He tells me all he sees. Thinks he sees.
A cloud, smoke drifting from the hostel
at Glencree; a bag caught in a fence,
someone waving in the distance. He waves.
Awakening in me forgotten memories.
Kindling in my cold bones, a father's
easily forgotten friendship for his son.

*from* This Far North
(1994)

# Penance

And still they live in unforgiven places,
on the sides of arthritic hills,
where low walls hide the sea and the sea
hides the dead, though the dead still whisper
in their silent graves, "I'm cold, I'm cold."

Enough bog here to stoke the fires of Hell,
and stones so many you'd think they grew
in the soil. Though nothing ever grows.
God knows there was more wood on Calvary.

This morning, on a high road beyond Cleggan,
I passed the ruins of a deserted cottage,
and a ruined cottage that looked deserted,
only a man eyed me. I asked where the road went?
"To the end," he said, "the end." Then shuffled off.

# Passion

After days of interminable rain,
light streams through the window.

You sit, just outside its gaze,
reading the Japanese –

the window, the light and you
making almost a perfect haiku.

Who would disturb the dust
settling on such quiet lines?

Only the breath from a bird's wings,
the movement of passionate hands.

# Preferences

I am fond of bicycles;
there is a great peace
in the shape of a wheel.

I like the way leaves
bend away from the sun
back toward the earth –
aware of the withering to come.

I like hills, rivers,
seas, woods.
I love the feel of stone
and the colour of grass.

And yet there are days
I drink for Ireland.

I am fond of books,
though not as fond as I used to be,
too many years in the woods
has turned my mind to heather and moss,
the occasional bluebell.

But I still like cigarettes
and Dylan songs,
favourite line – "I'm just whisperin'
to myself so I can't pretend that I don't know."

I love women.
I love the poetry of Akhmatova.
I love the full moon, its white host
against the black body of the sky.

And yet there are days
I drink for Ireland.

I like hands,
fingers in particular.
I love the shape of lips.
I love the way one testicle
hangs lower than the other,
typical of life's imbalance.

I love tea on cold November mornings.
And for some reason I've never
understood, I love islands
and all they encircle.
I love the pure poetry of Beckett.

I am gazing out the window
at three small islands
and two trawlers
ploughing out to sea.
It is the last day of April.
The sea is smooth as a feather.

But I prefer
when it goes berserk
like a salty drunk
and rages against Ireland.

# The Dreaming

*for* Patricia

*A man who has lost his dream
has lost his way.*
       – Aboriginal saying

If you stray from this road
you will be dead in a day.
If I had strayed I'd have
sung me a river and be tucked
in a hollow by nightfall.
I was the land and the land was me.

My world was sleeping until
my father dreamt the turtle
and the lizard. In his dream
I walked naked out of a lake
over the land towards the sea,
warmed always by the sun I sang.

Only at night I lit my fire
and painted my body,
following the lines of my bones
until I was a skeleton
dancing with the dead,
frightening away all evil.

And I kept it at bay
since the dawn of my dream,
until you came in disguise,
like me but not like me.
Your eyes stole my dream,
your tongue my song.

But you have no voice for singing
and you sleep too unsettled to dream.
Your needs and your thoughts imprison you.
You have the cold embrace of a stranger.
Even your God has banished you naked.
I pity you and you think you pity me.

# A Postcard from a Brothel in Singapore

Nothing happens here that
could not happen anywhere.
The three women in kimonos
sipping sweet tea, are
waiting to dazzle strangers.

They will tell your fortune
for five dollars. Sell you
cassettes, T-shirts,
watches for five dollars.
Everything else, bestowed
on them by Buddha,
is rounded off in fives.

The Madame squatting by the door,
is a small square-shouldered
woman so old she tells time
by the shadows on the floor.
She looks like a Door God
from a Hindu temple
only she wears no paint,
no jewels, and smells of heat.

This, they say, is the monsoon season.
It is a hundred degrees in the rain.
So what are we doing in a brothel
in Singapore? We are in the first
open doorway out of a downpour.

One look and I'm saying "Let's go!"
When Mary spots a payphone
on the wall and must get through

to her sister in Ireland
from a brothel in Singapore.

But since she began nattering
the cast from 'Genghis khan'
has lined up behind her
with handfuls of dollar bills
and excited looks in their almond eyes.

## These Hills

This morning a cloud crashed
on the slopes of my hills,
my breath on your breasts
on a cold winter's day.

I should have been weaned from these hills
twenty years ago.
I should have been,
for when you call me now

it is to gather in the shifting cows.
I'll tell you, love, if we're alone
and it's quiet, then more than likely
we're working on carrots or potato drills.

Sometimes you seem
like a woman waving
after the last boat moving
slowly out to sea, wave after wave.

But you're soft as a young river.
When I hold you close, your breasts,
your nipples are pressed to dark
rings like cats' eyes.

Oh, I still hold a cloud for you,
a ball of wool misted with blue.
But most nights find me clear of your soft
hills and just drifting towards sleep.

# Island Man in Paris

*i.m* Samuel Beckett

When I saw him last he was all dejection,
hands deep in the pockets of an old duffle –
he had a boatman's love of big hoods.
Living so far inland
he lacked a view of the sea,
though everything about him said islandman:

hair bleached white by the years at sea,
face chiselled by the salt in the wind.
Then those perfect blue eyes, set deep
to see through mist and spray. What hope
had eyes like these staring down narrow streets?
Everything crowding into them without perspective.

When I saw him last he was
standing amongst dust-bins.
"I'm old," he said, "I'm all used up.
I'm waiting to be collected."
"But Sam, there's no ships on the Rue St. Jacques."
"That's not strange," he said, "haven't you noticed,
there's no water. Only God's rain and our tears."

# When Sometimes all I Can Imagine are Hands

There is a winter within me,
a place so cold, so covered in snow,
I rarely go there. But sometimes,
when all I can imagine are hands,
when trees in the forest
look like they're made of wood,
then I know it's time
to take my photograph of Akhmatova
and sling it in a bag with socks and scarves.
My neighbours must think it strange
to see me strapping on my snowshoes,
to hear me roar at the huskies
as I untangle the harness.
But when all you can imagine are hands
it's best to give a little wave
and move out into the whiteness.

# Maddening Relations

*Yes, I loved her, it's the name I gave,*
*still give alas, to what I was doing then.*
– Samuel Beckett

I

I have mentioned them before:
the red bricks of the Asylum,
the comfort of the public house,

the coffin shapes of the windows
in our church, the black veil
my mother wore when she was dying.

It's not that I've the mind of a grocer,
given to gossip, I blame it on the wife
and her relations' relations,

their births, committals, burials.
The rutted paths of their lives.
There isn't a one of them that

doesn't know the exact times
of the buses from Dublin
to Portrane Lunatic Asylum.

II

Her aunt Maggie,
no, her aunt Joan.
No, Lily is the worst.

Moulded from an axe handle.
Face like a crucifix,
knuckles like rosary beads.

More worm than ploughed field.
Her coffin will collapse
before it enters the pit.

"Did you hear Michael was down
in Nelligan's Bar,
left like a man in a gale."

"Did you hear Michael was outside
chapel last Sunday.
How could he have heard the sermon?"

"I find Michael peculiar these days,
stays a lot in his fields.
I think there's a woman involved."


III

May Lily and her like rot in hell
for the flames they've brought into
my life; I was so happy as a boy.

Happy until the day I married,
or maybe the morning after;
I was so disappointed

between the sheets,
though it was the best
sleep I ever had.

Snored like a baby.
Dreamt of black breasted
girls in the Caribbean.


IV

Woke, years later, between
the drills of a potato field.
The chairs, the beds, the brooms,

the books, the house in ashes.
And you standing by the front wall
your face turned away crying.

Somewhere Lily was watching,
taking it all in like prayer.
The tongues of the village were clacking.


V

Here, in this room, by the mad
sea that swims to England,
I drift in memories.

My hand lifting another stone
the spade has turned over after
a thousand years of sleeping.

Rooks scurrying behind the plough,
meticulous as altar boys,
waiting for the worm to drop.

And you, that day you brought
your beauty into my fields,
your hair the colour of starlings.

In grey light I have spent hours
standing by the blessed door
waiting for the sound of your feet

to shiver in the puddles
at the bottom of the lane,
to echo into darkness.

All dissolves, like this tablet
on the end of my tongue, into nothing.
I pray to remember your face.

# Staying at the Big House

*for* Mary & Bernard Loughlin

> *Colm,*
> *Move your fucking jam-jar*
> *from in front of the house –*
> *The poets must be able to see*
> *the lake at all times.*
>                    Bernard

Poets, painters, playwrights haunt this house,
it is an eerie place to linger after dark.
My room looks out over a shadowy lake;
a cauldron of dreams for the banshee,
a dark well for the women of the wood.
At dusk I shutter my window against their spells,
turn my chair toward the fire and wait
for spirits to emerge from the walls,
to haunt the rooms with wails like the wind.
Last night I met the ghost of a girl upon the stairs.
She had pale blue eyes and pale blue hair.
As she swept through me, my bones were dipped
in ice – as if she had stolen a kiss from my soul,
and my soul had died for a moment to steal it back.

# Unveiling

### I

This could be Tuscany
but for the rain, the mist
and the hundreds of stone walls;
yesterday as I clambered over one
the whole lot came tumbling down on me.

You are gone only three days
and already I am bruised inside and out.

I miss your hands and their unveiling.

### II

They have begun a dig on Mooghaun Hill.
Three feet down the earth has revealed
the remains of an ancient hut,
its door, like ours,
facing away from the wind.

Hard to imagine that three feet
of leaves and dust have fallen
since someone last stood
in that doorway
waiting, as I do now, for the mountains
to define the shape and route of a woman.

III

Love, when you are home,
I will close this door
and though a thousand years of history
and a billion waning stars
are all around us,
we will sleep,
closer than feathers,
the breath of a kiss between us.

Archaeologists, digging for years,
might discover
that our house was here,
and our door faced away from the wind.
But what would they know
of the colour of your eyes,
how they darken in November?

# The Dowser and the Child

When you were leaving
I'd always asked if you
had brought an umbrella;
you made me think of rain
upon the hills. All our lives

there was a steady drizzle between us:
the sound of water in the distance.
Your hands, your eyes
dowsed over me, as if you
could divine things deep within me.

It seemed to me you moved beneath
a grey cloud. I remember,
even on sunny days, you wore
a great wide hat, your eyes
in darkness under the cool verandah.

Some days you were a passing shower.
Some days you were a snowflake.
Some days your tongue was a bolt
of lightning that sent me
scuttling under the kitchen table.

Hours I'd sit there, listening
to the thunder of your things
rolling in the distance.
Nights when the wind blew,
I could hear it moan in your room,

creaking the bed. If I opened the door,
you blew it shut with a shout.
Once when I was lost in the forest
at the back of our house, I followed
the cold wind that led home to you.

I ran down the path to embrace you,
but you stayed distant like all my
rainbows, and told me, and told me,
and told me, not to touch your
delicate colours with mucky hands.

# I am the Night Watch

Years of living like a badger
have left me blind in daylight,
but in darkness I see things
with a clarity that haunts me.

To pass the hours I do yoga or T'ai-Chi.
Sometimes I just sit and meditate
or let my spirit astral travel
about the factory. I've crystals

buried to warn me of intruders;
theirs is a dark force against my light.
I try to stay hidden in shadows,
but I fear my aura gives me away,

it's silver grey like a badger's coat
and glows with the yellow of my chakra.
Vera, a theosophist, say our chakras
are like small triangular train stations

where elemental forces in the body
converge – little carriages of light
that should be realigned once a year
or immediately after a tragedy.

Thankfully I've less of those
since I began leaving my decisions
to readings from the I Ching
and the turning of Tarot cards.

Vera thinks my nervous compatibility
with the night may spring from the fact
that I was a badger in a past life.
But then she also thinks I was an owl.

I think I was a tree in the darkest
of forests that borrowed daylight
through the leaves. Because often,
when I least expect it, I find

I miss the warm sun on my face
and the many colours of grass.

# Tea

*The only sanity is a cup of tea.*
                                    – Gwendolyn Brooks

I

Sometimes I think I'm drowning
in all the tea I drink,
that someday I'll be found
floating, face up,
on the surface of myself.
A coroner's report will read
"died of tannin poisoning,
horrendous discolouration
and distortion of the vital organs,
brought on by imbibing a lethal
cocktail of incredible brews."
I began, like most,
with teas from India, China and Ceylon,
but moved quickly on to Camomile, Mu,
Luaka, Rosehip, Hibiscus, Lemon Grass,
Cherry Stems, Orange Flowers, Blueberry Leaves,
Blackberry Leaves, Rose Buds, Linden Flowers,
a veritable hothouse of horrid herbal fusions.
Once, using the excuse that I was deeply in love,
I drank a fragrant mix of Passion Flowers,
Dandelion Leaves and Bancha Twigs,
I dream of a time when I can enjoy a Guinness
or something as cool and clear as a gin and tonic.

## II

My grandmother was also addicted.
The First World War caught her cold.
Tea rationed, she spent her days
recycling leaves or visiting friends.

With news of a second war
she moved my grandfather in
with the boys and filled his space
with boxes and boxes and boxes of tea.

For my grandmother
the First World War was hell,
but the Second was a marvelous
bit of gossip to have with a brew.

# The Coat

*i.m.* Osip Mandelstam

> *Are you a ghost, or a passing man,*
> *for some reason I preserve your shade.*
>          – Anna Akhmatova

The back of the chair now wears your coat,
it hangs as badly over its rickety frame
as it once did over yours. But on no other
chair does it look so well or remind me.

We were lame with the cold when they came
to arrest you; blue veins, like the rivers
of Europe, running over the backs of our hands.
Yet they stripped you down to the last word

and left me holding your empty coat.
I've replaced lost buttons, sewn the hem,
but I know you'll not be back for it
this winter nor the winter after.

To touch you now, I wrap your coat around me.
With my arms slipped into your arms,
and the belt pulled to the last notch,
I appear like your ghost returning.

# Northern Haiku

On an Antrim bog
a wall divides the wet land,
planted in the past.

Shot twice in the head.
Once in each astonished eye.
History is blind

Over the dark Foyle
the bark of Kalashnikovs,
an old Derry air.

Punishment shooting.
Pleads remorse and forgiveness.
Jeans gone at the knees.

Protestant prayers.
Popish prayers. Funerals.
We go the same way.

A man ploughing,
in one field he furrows from
Ireland to England.

A blackbird's sweet song
lost in the wildness of hills –
prayer for the dead.

# From a Famine Journal

I

*A list of exports leaving Cork harbour*
*On the 14th November 1848*

147 bales of bacon
120 casks of pork
135 barrels of pork
149 casks of miscellaneous provisions
1,996 casks of oats
950 barrels of oats
300 bags of flour
300 head of cattle
239 sheep
5 casks of ham
9, 398 firkins of butter
542 boxes of eggs

We watched it sail into a hungry wind.

1845

In her parlour, by a window that frames
the picture of a grey sky, Mrs. Elizabeth Wyatt
is polishing off an entry in her journal:
I've never seen Dublin so prosperous,
nor its fashions so exquisite.
Its straw bonnets are the best in Europe.
There's surely less misery than ever before.
And Mrs. Weaver's daughters, is there
anything so beautiful as delicate white hands?
We ate raised pies and ham, and apple tarts
with cream. Drank China tea all evening
from Mrs. White's white China cups.
This potato famine is greatly exaggerated.
In Dublin the Polka is all the rage.

### 1846

Today I travelled the whole estate
and saw little or no distress, just
two dead and a few cases of struggling.
The Irish are idle, impudent louts.
Dependent on those whom they so badly
abuse. No name seems too harsh for them.
So we have begun feeding our workmen,
thirty-two at present; half one day,
half the next. Charles killed a cow.
And the servants make a large pot of soup
which we serve each day at one.
Yesterday, I thought it such a pretty sight
to see everyone eating in the kitchen.

1847

Beyond the estate is a waste of misery.
There aren't the living to bury the dead.
I have watched them die in the ditches.
Seen them kneel down to curse their God.
No man, no woman, no priest, not even I
have the loaves and fishes to feed them.
And worse, the rags they wear barely
cover their decency. Even yesterday
when I called to see young Peggy Dodson,
whose husband and children have died,
she herself was almost naked and made no move
to cover her shame. I sleep badly these nights;
often, after undressing, I sit by the fire
reading or knitting petticoats for the wretched.

## 1847

Today I walked the back road home over the hill,
past farms that hadn't a hoof on their land.
Strange to say I saw no children in the lanes.
Some have been taken to relations in Dublin.
Four sheep and five cattle have been taken
from our land in the past month.
Having seen how some of the people die,
I hardly blame the wretches who steal.
But Charles is as mad as the Irish
and has employed three men from Dublin
to walk the fields at night with sticks and dogs.
I'm only surprised that such a superstitious race
aren't afraid to venture into darkness.
Even I wouldn't be found in the fields at night,
not with the ghosts of the terrible dead lurking.

## VI    WRETCHED CARGO

### 1848

This morning they sent thirty or forty
more convicts to the penal colonies.
Amongst them I saw, ironed and handcuffed,
the two Maguires whose mother I know well.
She has worked in the kitchen and was a
wet nurse when each of my children was born.
So I am ashamed to say she wasn't allowed
say goodbye to her sons, or even to touch
their hands, their faces, one last time.
The families of this wretched cargo
lined the road, their wives wailing.
And yet, miserable as these men looked,
I felt they were still better off
than the starved wretches waiting to hang.

1848

My husband says, "If this is the line
The Government and the Lords are taking
it would be better if they hanged them all
as most are so weak they'll not make it so far."
The vicar says, "The Maguire boys were drinking,
shouting for all who wanted to hear that
the new Commission was no better than if
the devil himself were trying to starve us."
Surely they should be forgiven such ignorance,
flayed even, or put to work on the roads,
not sent from the land like criminals.
I must send Mrs. Maguire the side of a lamb.
All this misery has again ruined Christmas
for everyone. I pray for a brighter new year.

1849

Many of the big houses and their estates
have come to the end of their lives.
The Barclays and the Hamiltons have fled.
Even Lady Dodd who had so much is leaving.
Bankruptcy, it seems, is overtaking us all.
Once the gates of an estate are closed
the house is gutted of its life. Everything
of value is stolen, and sold for passage to America.
They're saying they have found gold in California.
That a man can earn forty pounds a day.
Here the wages, for those who can find work,
are three pence a day. But the good news is
we had new potatoes at dinner, floury and dry.

1849

Though there is cholera in Dublin I steeled myself
and went to see the young Queen promenade.
For many the day was spoilt by torrential rain,
but I was more distressed to see her grown so fat.
Her dress was far too plain, her skin almost dark.
Though the papers have her down as beautiful.
I suspect some poor man is bound to lose his job
for the terrible misprint in the second column:
"The Queen pissed over the bridge". I am ashamed
to say I held my breasts and rudely laughed.
On the way home we passed a family of five
dead in a ditch. It seems the cholera is spreading
towards the mountains. But worse news was awaiting
our arrival, the blight has appeared on our potatoes.

1850

We docked last week in Sydney after eight months
at sea and left a ship I had grown to abhor.
I doubt I will ever get over the shame of undressing
and washing in front of other women. But worse,
what youth I had I left in Ireland ravaged by
famine, cholera and five wretched years of misery.
Sadly, we buried Lady Hutton and Mr. Vicars at sea.
Though I doubt they would have liked it here.
There is a nearness in the sun's heat.
I was saddened to hear that convicts and soldiers
and farmers are still clearing the land of natives.
After a life of such worry, it's a great relief to be opening
a hotel in the city for respectable ladies and gents
or as Charles says, "The new Australians like ourselves".

*from* Three Songs of Home
(1998)

# Redeemed

*for* Michael Hartnett


After years in the quietest of rooms
I have taken to the road again.
God, in his wisdom,
has left everything unblessed:
the withering trees; the bracken
that covers the bones of winter;
the hawthorn, the blackthorn;
the stone walls gone to ruin;
the mongrel ditch, the culled fields.
I place myself amongst them
and feel at home.

# All the Mountains

### I

I have lived all my life
staring out this window
at the mountains of Mourne,
and not until this moment
did they even appear remotely
like the Himalayas,
but there they are now
washed in the magnificent light
of those Eastern peaks.

Is it because at this moment
some burly little man
wrapped in a yak skin
is whistling
*The Mountains of Mourne?*
or muttering to himself
like a small hill farmer:

"If I had two more beasts
I could marry in June,
then my bed would be
a shelter in the winter nights?"

### II

I've seen monasteries in the Himalayas
held to the sides of mountains
by snow and the grace of prayer,
and trees adorned with ribbons
that look like lanterns from the valley,

and in the valley walls made
like those you'd find in Connemara.
Yet, though it is bleak in winter,
and it is always winter,
Tibetans are kind people.
As you pass they wave.
Proud of their cleared land
and their hard work,
they stare after you
until you are out of sight,
leaving you wondering
if they are staring still.


### III


I have heard that if you die
in the Himalayas in winter,
the earth being frozen –
too hard to dig –
your body is placed on stones
until the bones are picked clean
by birds of prey.
Then the skeleton is gathered
and divided amongst the relatives:

the skull for the mother,
the hands for the father,
the feet for a holy man.

IV

A Lama once told me
there are no ghosts in the Himalayas.
All Heaven might be here,
I thought, and he'd never know,
everything being covered
in cloud, mist and snow.
But then, as if reading my eyes,
he said, "There are no ghosts
because no one ever dies.

A year after we buried my father
a yak came to the monastery.
I though it a hairy nuisance,
and went to shoo it from the gate,
but I saw my father in its eyes;
I fed him and blessed him
and he went away.

Here everything, from the marks
on these hands to the hairs
on a dog's tail, is reincarnated:
rain returns as rivers,
snow as mountains,
birds as holy Lamas.
Women rarely die:
deep rivered valleys
and high mountains
mirror their lives.
Children come back
as birds that sing in the wind.

This close to Heaven
even rainbows are the souls
of holy men evaporating."

He took my hands in his
and uttered a quiet prayer:
a shield of grace to cover my cold
soul. Then I watched him move
slowly off down the valley, until
his saffron robes fluttered open
and a bright bird's wing
lifted him into the mist.


        v


That night, staring out the window
of a Sherpa's hut,
I learned the beauty of a mantra:
*Kantega, Nuptse, Tawchee, Lotse,*
*Ama Dablam, Annapurna, Chomolungma,*
*Carrauntoohill, Maumturk, Mourne.*
I blessed the mountains,
while the mountains blessed me.

## Still Life

When I heard of the Tibetan
who made a clock and then
destroyed it because it would be
yet another distraction,
I wondered:

Was he troubled by the ticking?
Was he worried he'd never
be quite sure whether to place it
on the shelf or by the bed?
Maybe he felt he'd always
be getting up to glance
at its slowly changing face
or to settle the hands.

So why did he make the clock?
Was it to see if time moved?
And then – suddenly –
at the first tick, it did,
and he began to wonder:
How long do I work?
What's it take to walk from one
end of the valley to the other?
Does day pass quicker than night?

I can see him now, that quiet man,
stepping away from the table,
taking a deep, slow breath,
as he lifts the hammer and swings
so that the cogs, and the ticking,
and the time, vanish in a moment.

# In Darjeeling

When the old Lama looked
curiously at me,
I thought it was to ask
why I hadn't touched
my yak-butter tea,
or what I thought the hands
of God might be holding
at this hour of the day.
Instead he asked,
in his faltering English,
why Americans found
the mountains so extraordinary.
"They're different," I said.
"Like me they find them
mystical places."
"Oh," he said, "and I thought
they were all circling fools.
When I pass them on the hills
they always say 'High!'
And 'Yes,' I say, 'Very High,'
and promise myself
to light a candle
for their circling souls."
"Father," I said, shaking my head,
"they say 'Hi!' and mean 'Hello!' "
He looked thoughtful for a moment.
"I think I have wasted
a thousand prayers
on a hundred kind greetings.
God must be laughing at Lama Doshi."

# Air

Parts of this country are like County Clare:
the old stone walls, the ghosts in the wind.
I might nearly be happy living here,
but what I miss in the evening is salt in the air.

I was raised on a small northern island.
There're days I like to stand looking at waves,
grey sky falling as far as the eyes can see.
When I told all this to Lama Doshi, he said:

"Ah yes, you might nearly be happy living there,
but what you'd miss in the morning is a great
mountain, something to take the bare
look off the sky, the sadness out of the air."

# Prayer Guide

The beads Lobsang uses to count his prayers
are made from the bones of his father's hands.

Each time he comes to the end of a prayer, he slips
a piece of smooth white bone through his fingers

then begins his chant all over again;
his father's hand still guiding the way.

# Hat

One evening, after he'd finished praying,
I asked Lama Doshi if he liked poetry.
"I never read it," he said, "but I love
when it greets me on the street.

This morning I spent hours arguing
with Mr. Ho about the price,
and the meaning, of a new hat:
he knows I choose my own cloth.

This year I wanted none
of his Chinese greys and blues.
I wanted a hat with gold, purple,
saffron, the yellow of a butter-cup,

the red of a dragonfly:
so that even a stranger,
passing at a distance,
could see the poet in me."

# The Damned

*A lovely day!*
*Ah yes! But we'll pay for it.*
— An Irish greeting

"I brought seven young monks
to see you last night," Lama Doshi said.
"You couldn't have, I was in
all evening, pottering about."

"I only brought them to see you," he said,
"we stood outside and looked through the window.
They were curious to know how a man
*eternally damned* copes in the silence.

I had told them you believe you will
burn forever after your last breath.
Some thought it eerie the way you leaned
over the fire as you read your book.

On the way home we discussed the sin
for which you might be damned.
Most thought you must have killed a man,
but Dimsang, the boy you know well,

he suggested: you are probably damned
because you are a vain, unholy poet
who lives outside the moment
and in that place, always for yourself.

Thinking on this and on Buddha's teachings,
they agreed with Dimsang and were content.
Then they sang healing songs for you,
and I recited sacred poems to comfort your soul."

# The Journey Home

*i.m.* Augustine Canavan

Some mornings
from my window
I can hear,
high up in the mountains,
the bell the monks ring
to call them to pray
for who they were,
who they are,
and who they will become,
on the journey home.

And some mornings
I join them in prayer,
imagining my own journey:
how far I've travelled
with so much baggage.
But the higher I've climbed
into the mountains,
the more I have discarded.

Let me tell you why I've come
to this ledge on a mountain,
this window on the snow-line:
it is to meet the ghost
who lives inside of me,
a man or woman I have not
seen for centuries, whose face,
whose voice, whose touch

I have forgotten,
but who knows my fear.
This soul who holds a bell for me,
that, at my last breath,
he'll ring to guide me.

# Now that I am Almost Dead

Now that I am almost dead
the ghosts in corridors
hold no fear for me.
I feel I know them.
They are teaching me to whisper,
to listen to others' conversation
as if I am not there. To leave
and enter rooms unnoticed; to fade.
And I can feel a ghost growing inside me.
What is hard is the loneliness,
the learning to live without dreams.

I walk the rooms at night
while others sleep,
knowing the skin that fits me now
will never fit so well again,
that my blue eyes will fade,
that my voice will soon be quiet.
And if I could wish,
it would be that when I die
your ghost still floats inside me,
and we haunt these rooms together,
or sleep eternally under a mountain,
the clay our blanket.

# A Habitable Place

*There is no place on earth where death cannot find*
*us – even if we constantly twist our heads in all*
*directions as if in a dubious and suspect land.*
— Montaigne

Reach inside of me;
through the clay, through the forest,
deep into clouds.
Open me; there's only sky,
one restless bird flying west.

~

All winter I dreamt
of a habitable place
to melt skin on skin;
lovers held warm as feathers,
cradled from the curse of ice.

~

The sky was empty
when they found the dead blackbird;
a sort of singing
gone forever with the wind.
Pray for us who have no wings.

~

Another evening
waiting for the light to die;
gone, almost grey now.
If I liken you to cloud
there is no sky can hold you.

~

The grave still open,
all its crumbling earth still damp,
and my mother's breath,
cold as the trees in winter,
frozen on her last word: 'home'.

~

No gift for talking.
Yet she'd hear the dead whisper:
a sea of stories;
where they lived or where they died;
chatter of distant voices.

~

I wake in the night,
my mother's voice at my ear,
a river of sighs.
Darkness, the oddest country,
ghosts more living than the dead.

~

Must have been so old.
Must have heard other voices
and thought them the wind.
When I go down on my knees
the dust rises with my voice.

~

When the dust settled
I was sitting by the window
watching her dead hands;
colour was gone from her face,
as if her ghost frightened her.

~

I have seen her ghost,
drawing itself on the road,
in search of its grave:
testing each six feet of earth,
the north wind cold in her eyes.

~

And when the snow falls
the hills curl in on themselves
and the rivers freeze.
You open and close your door
as if birds are in the air.

~

If death is a stone,
the haunted live in rivers,
gaze through fishes' eyes,
and though they cry in the night
they are not blessed with voices.

~

The cross of evening
spreading out like a dark bird:
moon eyed, star feathered;
bright creature of this dark night –
you and I afraid of flight.

~

You told me of death,
said I'd climb to grasp its breath;
that I'd utter prayer;
that I'd carry my own soul
before I sank into earth.

# The Crossing

After the yaks came the porters
with winter in their voices;
they told of passes frozen to the North.

But we were waiting for horses
before making the crossing,
for we had old men and books
and other slow, heavy things to carry.

The wind was up and it was bitterly cold,
yet all the signs were still right:
the yaks' eyes were clear,
the dogs faced into the wind.

It would be, at least, another week
before snow covered the lower passes,
and our journey no more than a day.

But the horses never came,
and the yaks' eyes closed,
and the dogs turned around,
and the road was gone.

The porters, settling in for the winter,
when they weren't sipping tea
or praying "Om Mani Padme Hum!"
had another story to tell

of how winter stole in early
and changed the life of every traveller

who left it late to make the simple crossing
from the warmth of one doorway to another.

"Not a story, more a prayer,"
I heard one of the old men say.

# Lobsang's Wife

For over half the year I live with ice
on the river, yet ice on the river
is something I've never understood –

*water asleep on water*
*is not washed*
*away.*

And on days when cloud covers the valley
I light a candle in the window,
hang sage on the door.

Lobsang,
vanishing into the mist,
says I am no more than a child.

Let him talk and curse;
for what if the cloud lifted
while he was inside its body?

Who then would mend his bones?
Bless his eyes? Who then would hear
the last words of his mantra? Listen,

as I get older what I love are the mornings
when the sky clears to a deep blue
and I can see as far as mountains days away.

There are times Lobsang goes there.
Nights I should miss his voice in the room,
his face by the fire. I tell you, this time

when he returns from the hills,
I'll take his hands in mine,
and though he may

rush for his prayer wheel,
stomp like a yak,
curse me for a wife,

I'll ask him
then and there,
what's this snow that covers our lives?

# Blue Bowl

*for* Paula Meehan

What she did
with all the blue bowls
I was never too sure,
but every time she went away
she brought one home.

When I visited,
I noticed she put
nothing in them,
and she did not
use them on the table.

I never asked her
about the bowls
for fear of offending
some tradition
I did not know about.

But this morning
I mentioned them
to her husband,
Lobsang,
and he said,

"When she started
to gather them,
I too was intrigued.
So, one day,
I asked her.

*Use them!* She said,
*isn't each one filled*
*to the brim*
*with the memories*
*of a pilgrimage?*

She pointed to a bowl:
*That contains*
*the first days of spring,*
*and every step from here*
*to the monastery at Rongbuk.*

*And this, this tiny blue*
*bowl, is late autumn*
*on the road to Namche;*
*many icy days*
*and long dark nights."*

And did you find out
why they are always blue?
"Yes, but not from her.
On a pilgrimage of my own
I asked an old Lama.

She chooses a blue bowl
so it won't be out of place
with the others, or seem
somehow more important
when it's filled."

# Bread

### I

All evening I had watched
the women of the house
knead dough into snowy mounds,
white as the mountains around us;
their floured hands placed a great
calmness in the air –
like incense in a temple.
I loved the way they folded
each loaf in a prayer
before placing it by the fire, to rise.

### II

I was sleeping in the kitchen
when the ghost of an old woman
came from the shadows and stood
by a window filled with stars.
I wanted to ask her
why she was still stirring
when her breath was gone
but something in the air
told me – quieten.
I watched as she folded
an apron about her,
then set to making bread

with the same tucks and folds
I'd seen the other women make.
And as I watched
her floured hands bless the air

it began to dawn on me
that this was why
even in the middle of the night
the house smelt of bread.

# Lobsang's Last Wish

Lobsang loves the smell
of things. He says,
when you are dying
it is the last of the senses to leave.

So, on that particular day
he will fill the room
with all the wildflowers
that grow along the riverbank.

Then, when the other senses
are gone, when the eyes
are blind, when the room
is hushed, when the pain

is so great he won't
even remember
to remember
to pray,

in that darkness,
the smell of a yellow
petal might bring
him back long enough

to give thanks for such
small blessings,
and die a grateful
rather than a bitter man.

# Ch'a

– *after* Ho

*Everything great on earth
begins as something small.*
– Lao Tzu


I

Older than China
I am the memory of trees;
sip the earth from me.

I remember mist,
sunlight climbing the steep hills
leaf by silent leaf.

When I was a seed
I was drawn to a raindrop:
we made a strange brew.

Take me in silence;
I am all of the autumn,
cup me in your hands.

Warm in your fingers,
I am moments of quiet in
long conversations.

More than a prayer
on the road with the pilgrims,
by windows in rain.

**II**

And if you see yourself here,
hand lifting the cup,
imagine these are your leaves:

no curse this winter, then spring,
three months of sadness,
you'll see its shadows haunting.

The house will feel empty, but
then there is passion,
cups left on the floor. Sunlight.

# Stillness

On still nights I hear
the songs my grandmother sang:
three sad songs of home.

# The Voyage

It is years since I last crossed
by boat to Ireland,
but tonight I am going home
over the waves.
The sky is filled with fading stars,
their light has travelled for a million years
and they are weary; the last trace
of the light that left us here.

I had promised to be in Dublin by summer
but it is the first of November,
the first day of winter.
The decks are icy underfoot
and there is snow in the air. Behind me,
a man is asking a woman if she loves him.
It is far too cold for such great questions.
It is an Irish night, under an Irish sky.

And I am beginning to remember this voyage:
the beer, the songs, the cigarettes;
the asthmatic wheeze of the engine
as it lifts us over another mountainous wave.
It is all up hill to Ireland:
against the tide, against the wind,
against the dark and the cold.
The journey, preparing us for the land.

# A Quiet House

Since I've moved to the hills
I've stopped sleeping naked,
but taken to planting flowers;
not just in the garden
but in cooking-pots, buckets,
any old containers.
This year, when you return,
there will be laburnum, iris,
seven types of fuchsia,
to waken to each morning.
And I make this promise to you now:
I have done with travelling.
I am mending the wood
in the window, the tap at the sink.
I am letting the clocks run down.
This time, the house will whisper
when you sleep, and it will take, at least,
nine hours of moonlight to waken you.

*from* What Darkness Covers
(2003)

*Tonight my love's eyes*
*are the colour of the sea*
*and I wish to drown.*

*It is way past midnight.*

*I am writing*
*by lamp light, darkness*
*lapping at my feet.*

# Blind

Now when I call, she says,
"Step close and let me see you."
She lifts her fingers onto my face,
then up over my eyes so I go blind.

I smell the lavender on her hands,
the ash in the grate, cat smell, church smells,
turf and apple-mint. An apron hung to dry.
The smell of the yard on boots by the door.

And beyond the door, the weather:
rain and mist. Earth-smells:
cattle and woodburn. The dead leaves
at the dead end of the year. And all

through the wood the whirling wind,
the open wing, eggshell and birdsong,
and mosses from the riverbank
smelling of frog and flick of fish tail.

Then, as she lifts her fingers
releasing my eyes back into the light,
"You're looking well," she says,
and asks for news of weather and the day.

# What Darkness Covers

Because I cannot sleep
and you are far away,
this dishevelled bed
holds no dreams,
and blankets and darkness
cover only emptiness.
I look where you should be
but you are utterly gone.
I lie remembering.

My grandmother used to say
the dead love this time of year;
the nights so long
they walk amongst us whispering.
This morning I found
footprints on the path,
tears on every leaf.
*Listen, is that a door opening*
*Or a door closing?*

Old Italians used to say
the most beautiful sculpture
Michelangelo ever made
was a snowman
in the Boboli Gardens:
a male nude chiselled out of ice,
you could see where his soul
was held. He turned all to tears
and was washed away.

I do this all the time,
try to hold on.
Sometimes I feel
I am the last leaf on the tree,
and there will be no rest
until I fall. So I say –
Let everything that falls, fall;
beginning with tired love
and ending in the old way:

*the eyes still,*
*the breath gone,*
*all quiet until*
*the earth's rain falls.*

# Another Room

This was our room.
It has four walls,
I counted them
when you left:

the one with the door,
the one with our pictures,
the one with the window,
the one with our bed.

But now, to put away the memory
of how your hands, your mouth
turned my skin into electricity,
I have taken myself away.

I have moved to another room.
It too has four walls,
but the door opens to the other side,
and there are no pictures of you.

And in the dark,
when I bury your ghost,
the memory of your touch
goes out with the light.

# Juliet Sleeping

Unused to a baby
in the house,
the grandmother
has emptied turf
from a creel
and filled it with
soft cotton sheets.
Now Juliet sleeps
in a wicker bed,
dreaming of moss.

"And not just moss,"
the grandmother says,
"but all of the woods,
the light and the half-light,
for it is late autumn
and this child is dreaming
the brown into her eyes."

# Masterplan

God made today
as he will make tomorrow,
as he made yesterday.

He has been doing this
year in, year out
for as long as I can remember.

The only thing he changes
is the weather
and how he moves

the people under the clouds:
some he brings into the world,
some he takes away.

He works magic with flowers,
miracles with water,
sorcery with stars.

He does this and that
and hallelujahs,
and bucketfuls of sadness.

What he does with love
and hate is a *tour-de-force:*
in a moment he can

break or mend you heart.
He assures us in his book
he has a masterplan,

that every step is neatly mapped,
from the sorrow of whale song
to the shyness of the platypus.

But all I want from him
is to slow
the whole thing down

so I can at least appreciate
all the work he has put in,
covering up the cracks.

## Still Life with Books

Most mornings I wake early
as if I have somewhere to go,
something to do. I potter
for an hour through books,
papers, photographs.

Then I sit by the window
for the rest of the day.

And if there is rain,
*I fish for tears.*
And if there is mist,
*I sift for ghosts.*
And if there is snow,
*I chisel for stars.*

In between
I pace the room
or watch the gate
for the comfort
of the postman. How
did I end up like this?

A watcher of skies
and fields that run to clouds;
a keeper of stillness,
a moonface at the window,
a love gone to darkness,
a still life with books.

# Nude

She has been with me all winter.
I cannot say I hate her
for when I was young
I loved everything about her.
There were nights
I could have died for her.
Now there's an awful
pattern to our lives.

She arrives late September
carrying sacks of old books,
and pinned to her dress
or tied in her hair,
or buried in the folds
of her skin,
are those few new poems
I have waited all summer to hear.

But each year her price
goes a little higher
and I grow weary.
Often she undresses
to the bone:
peeling her skin,
folding the wrinkled
hide over the bed
where she sups and stares.

Often she strips me too,
planting the tips
of her fingers
like roots in my eyes,

or pushing her tongue
deep into my mouth.
Bare. Naked. Nude.
Unless you've ever
served her,
felt her cunning
on your lips,
you'll never know
the meaning of the word.

And yet,
one of these mornings
I'll find her
standing in the kitchen
dressed for the road,
coat, hat, scarf,
bags tied with string,
and I'll be on my knees
begging her to stay.

# The Long Rest

Late autumn. They are taking the dead
from the church and bringing them
up to the field at the back of the town
where they will leave them forever.

It has put me in mind of the day
my grandfather retired.
Kathleen and Carmel, the daughters
who lived with him at home,

had cooked rashers and sausages,
baked sweet apple tart, had the
kettle on the stove, ready to scald
the leaves when they heard the gate.

Half-past-six, the same as every other day,
the latch was lifted, the bicycle stored
and my grandfather came in from work
to rest by the fireside forever.

He took from his waistcoat the silver
pocket watch he had been given,
told the girls he'd done well,
then handed them each a brown envelope.

Vouchers for Clery's?
Tickets to the Olympia?
No, my grandfather
was a practical man.

He had bought them a place in the shade
of a yew, up at the back of the town,
a bed for the long rest –
for each daughter, a grave.

# Baffled

*for* David Crook

Like you, I have spent
most of my life baffled.
No sooner does the light
dawn than it's dark again.
There are times I wonder
why I get out of bed
to traipse the streets
like a familiar ghost
heading for the fruit market.
How can bananas
become somebody's life?

And before this,
when I lived in the
grave-digger's cottage,
she said my skin
always smelt of the dead.
Six feet down,
level with their bones,
I could hear them sighing.
Mid-winter, I'd swear
their eyes were watching.
Fewer died over Christmas,
most panted on until
the new year, gave
out crossing the line.
*What did you get
for Christmas? A grave.*

The Parish Priest
would call down
"Make sure you
square the edges.
Nothing settles out
a life better than
a smooth descent."
His own went as easily
as the tide turning.
I can still remember
my surprise at how
upset she was. As they
lowered the coffin
she began to cry.
I though at first
it was a seagull.

Living close to the shore
they were always on at me
to go to sea. But though
I loved an old dip, the sea
is something else
that has always baffled me:
it goes up, it goes down.
It come in come, it goes out,
like a drunk's friendship
with his favourite bar.
And then for no reason
other than a freshening breeze
or a scrap of cloud,
it flies into a rage

and spits stones.
Bad weather, and the boats
could be tied up for weeks.
*If you want me I'll be in the bar.*

Strange that when you are young
she lies before you
like a floozie.
You suck and swallow
suck and swallow
until thirty years later
you stare across
the table at the shadow
keeping you company
and say: *One of these days
I must give this up.*
He laughs and gets in
another round
and the world spins on.

We live for what we love
and wait for death.
Surely love and death
are the two great shrines
to the bewildered.
I am a disciple of one
heading towards the other,
bothered that life
is not a tightrope
along which we edge
in our own creaky fashion,

but something tossed away
by a famished god,
a banana skin awaiting
the heel of another
hapless pilgrim.

# Found Poem

*A man on the radio talks about*
*how he's lived to be 100 years old.*

"I met her when she was seventeen.
She used to sing in the Choir;
one of those voices close to angels.

She was always younger than me.
A small, beautiful woman,
she turned heads on the street

and my heart on the pillow.
Dead seven years now, seven dead
years – I sleep with her ghost.

I put this long life
down to taking time
to make and drink, love and tea."

# Jimmy

*For who can bear to feel himself forgotten.*
    – W. H. Auden

That old soldier
he still comes round
every odd Tuesday afternoon.
He brings a glass eye,
a useless arm,
and all the war
that lingers on his skin,
a withered heart.
And yet, Jimmy
has the gentlest soul
I've ever known;
it's just he could never
climb out of the trench
they left him in.

These days he shuffles
when he walks
and his good hand shakes:
dampness gone to the bone.
Last night,
stroking my breasts,
he said the tips of my nipples
were smooth as bullets.
Then the air went silent,
as if we were waiting
for shells to fall.
I looked at him
sprawled naked,

a wounded man.
And I saw tears,
saw the glass-eye
like a sheet of ice
covering a flood.

# Currach

This is my boat.
I made it
with my own hands.
I took salt
from a bitter wind,
hair from
a horse's mane,
thread from
a woman's blouse.

Three stories
my father told me.
The sideways look
my mother has
when she is
curious and alone.
Her silent prayers.
A few rusty nails
from the kitchen door.

Three views of the island:
one in mist, one in rain,
one rocking in a drunken sea.
No flowers.
My people
had no love of leaves,
they saw boats in trees;
now the boats are gone
And the hills are bare.

At night, I sowed
curses into the oars,

rubbed fish oil
into the wood,
for I knew the journey
that lay ahead.
My people's story
was written on water.
Most of it is washed away.

My grandfather
knew the tale
but he'd not tell it.
His ghost sits
in the stern
saying:

*The future
is a steady course,
row strongly.*

*from* Poems After Paintings by Lucian Freud

PORTRAIT

There are naked portraits
and naked portraits,
but this
is a truly naked portrait.

One of my knees is up
so high it covers my breast,
the other is spread
to open me like a flower.

Curled on a bed,
I could be a woman
who has just given birth,
the loss still on her face.

Or I might be a baby
in the womb –
writhing like a fish,
slithering for the first time.

Or maybe I am
a captured soul,
tortured and abused,
a victim, somebody's prey.

But then, spread
on this white sheet
I might as easily be an Eskimo
listening at an ice-hole

for a seal's breath.
Or in my skin, a seal
under the ice, listening
for an Eskimo's footsteps.

Or maybe I am simply
what I seem, a woman
on a bed after love-making –
neither here nor there –

her man, trailing excuses
gone to make tea and toast.
The only thing I'm certain of
is I am changed:

painted like this, it is
as if my soul
has been tattooed,
branded, nailed to the wall.

NUDE WITH LEGS

A nude woman
sits in an attic door
legs dangling above
a confession box,
basking in sinshine.

DARK CHOCOLATE

Here's how I like it:
sweet, melted over nipples,
mouthfuls at a time.

BIG

It wasn't that I was always big.
It wasn't that at four years of age
I began eating only doughnuts.

It's something in me:
an old ache, not heartache,
but something like neglect.

The year would turn
and every summer
I'd be bigger than before.

And then this man
stops me in the street
saying he'd like to paint me, nude.

Pervert, I thought
and so old
with mean eyes,

skinny as a whippet.
I asked him to leave me alone
or take himself back to the home.

But a week later he called to my hatch –
I'm a benefit supervisor –
with photos of his work.

They were nothing like I'd seen
before: men and women naked
but dressed, living in their skin.

Six months I sat for him
in his studio
on the Marylebone Road.

Now I'm up on the wall
in the new Tate,
for everyone to see.

When I go to see myself
people always point
and the guard winks.

I sometimes wonder
what my mother
would have made of me.

I suppose she wouldn't
have minced her words.
But I think, naked

I look glorious.
Look at me:
I look like a woman

taking a bath without water.
A saint burning without flames.
A bird opening its wings.

I look through a painter's eyes.
I look like I never looked before,
and yet, exactly the same.

THE BATEMAN SISTERS

Between the red flowers and the yellow flowers,
in a garden as long and warm as last December,
in a suburb of Fremantle, Western Australia,
the Bateman sisters sunbathe nude. They do this
every sunny day, and here every day is sunny.
Eva is twenty-one or two and Bella, with the
mauve birthmark on her breast, a little older.

Pablo Neruda and Robert Graves
would have rejoiced in them as muses;
Lucian Freud would have brought
their souls to the edge of their skin;
Rodin, moulded them in bronze;
Andy Warhol, canned them.

So what is it in me that cannot celebrate
their beauty, that looking out this window
feels only disquiet and regret?
The grey pieties of a damp grey island.
I'd love to write a poem about how natural,
how beautiful the Bateman sisters are.

But I cannot get away from that boy
trapped in the coldness
of a Christian Brother's classroom:
*All flesh is sin.*
*Your body is a temple.*
*A woman's curves are the Devil's tools.*

To write unfettered by the Indian Ocean
in the heat of this blue day
I'd need to undress
and shed a lifetime of Irish rags.

NAKED GIRL WITH EGG

Up to this he always painted me
as just a naked model upon a sheet.

But a while ago he began adding
two fried eggs (sunny side up).

I thought he was enjoying a joke;
the eggs so similar to my breasts.

As he painted it dawned on me,
the eggs were my ovaries;

all I meant to him
was the cold white dish.

# Petrarch's Wife

In a dreary suburban maisonette
the reincarnation of Petrarch's wife,
or the woman who should have been his wife,
has declared war on the sugared sonnet.

Instead of slender hands and long black hair
she's taken burnt-out cars and wheelie-bins,
and woven them with malicious care
into the Dublin prattle of her lines.

I called last night, but a message says:
"Too busy in the sonnet mines
to come to the phone right away,
but if you leave your name and fourteen lines,
or good rhymes for cider, condom, chip-van
I'll get back to you as soon as I can."

# Mountain Woman

When he came home
I had crammed the garden
with cardboard boxes;
a neighbour had told me
they could break a fall.

I had nets over the windows,
a trampoline out the back.
I clung to the kitchen door
and would not use the stairs.
I ditched my handbag and

began wearing a parachute.
When I sat, I sat on
cushions. When I slept,
I slept on a mattress
on the floor.

And then last night he asked,
"Are you expecting to fall?"
"Yes," I said, "I have been
climbing since I met you,
and it is a long way down.

Now the air is so thin
I am always afraid;
it is hard to breathe.
For the last few days
I've been clinging to this ledge.

But you see nothing,
all you do is moan about
a shambles of nets and boxes.
I used to think it was all
a question of balance.

That once I was tied to you
I'd be safe. When I'd climb,
you'd climb. When I fell,
you'd fall. But now I know
it is the fear of falling alone,

with nothing
or no one
to catch me,
that keeps me holding on,
and I need so much to let go."

# Olympians

Next up are the poets.
This was never going
to be a glorious race
but after the pandemonium
of the heats
let's at least make sure
they're all facing the same way.

Running in lane one
in anonymous and fragments,
with a withered arm
and a halt leg,
it's the Greek beauty Sappho,
all sandy smiles
and dark brown eyes,
it's rumoured
she moves like the wind.

Beside her, in lane two,
with the haiku –
seventeen steps
of grace and precision –
it's the butterfly
of the short line,
representing Japan,
the little man, Basho.

In three with the sonnet
is William Shakespeare,
his run will depend
on impeccable rhythm,
on getting it all to flow.

Though a shadow is cast
over his selection
with Percy Shelley,
William Wordsworth,
Samuel Coleridge
and George Gordon, Lord Byron
all testing positive for opiates.

In lane four
with the villanelle
it's the Welshman Dylan Thomas:
after a lifetime of injuries
and unfulfilled promise –
it's marvellous to see him
finally up on his feet.

In the middle of the field,
standing out like a king,
is the long-distance legend,
blind Homer from Greece.
Kit Smart was a contender, but
he never turned up for the race.

Beside him,
crammed into six,
are Dante –
the Italian wizard,
the antelope of terza rima –
and a couple of farm boys,
Frost and Heaney.
I've seen them in practice,
they move with deceptive ease.

In lane seven, in the four
by four hundred relay,
it's the Russian champions –
they pass the baton
with silk-like grace –
Pasternak to Tsvetayeva,
Tsvetayeva to Mandelstam,
Mandelstam to Akhmatova.
She brings it home
with tremendous power
and gritty determination.

Out in lane eight,
going round the bend,
there's an army of poets.
I recognise at least a hundred
faces preparing for the start.

And then,
not with a shot
or a shout,
but with a collective sigh,
they're off.

It is poetry in motion,
like something out of Brueghel
the stillness is absolute,
for no one has moved.

They have closed their eyes
and are imagining
the wind on the face
the sweat on the brow
the pain in the chest
the ache in the heart
the hardship
the loneliness
the grief
that has brought them to this.

Some are already
closing on the line.
Others will take
hours, days, weeks, months.
Some will still be running
when the crowds are gone
when the lights are off
when the stadium's closed.

And some will
never make it home:
their words, their faces,
their lives forgotten.
They will turn to dust
where they fall.
The earth takes back
what it gives away –
the lanes run on forever.

# The Boat

Now that I have come this far there is no
    turning back.
And yet, what if there is nothing at the end
    of the track?

What if there is only more rock and sea?
    What if when
you open your eyes there's still the interminable
    grey rain?

Will you take it out on me? Or will you say:
    Let us make our bed here.
Winter approaches and we need food
    and shelter.

For even in this emptiness we have each other.
    We are from the same mould,
close as body and soul, feather and air, fish
    and water, rain and wind.

And brushing the hair from your face, will you
    take my hand and place it on
your breast saying: How were you to know
    the boats would leave so soon?

How were you to know the boats were here at all?
    So, let me settle.
Cities have been built by men like you,
    waiting for the boat home.

# Now Winter's Over

I've been told this winter's nearly over,
so I'd like to give thanks to you, O Lord,
and if not you, then to whoever
led me through; for someone
kept me still under tumbling skies,
warm even on the darkest days.

Now, as she retreats, I watch her fold
her blanket of leaves in the field,
load her wagon with boxes of frost,
sheaves of ice, rolls of mist, barrels of rain.

Her last act will be
disposing of her enemies
caught like lambs in the briars –
the crows will pluck out their eyes.

From an open window
I'll watch green leaves
lick the blood from raindrops,
coax the life out of sunbeams,

suck till the smell of spring fills the air:
*the cries of children in streets*
*the crackle of yellow crocuses*
*the eyes of leaves opening on trees.*

If it weren't for the rest
of this dishevelled world,
I'd almost dare to say
I am happy to be alive.

# Three Remedies

*from* The Magical Book of Winter Cures

And this is the first of the healing cures,
the oldest remedy, the most often used –
it is of course for the broken hearted.
They come trailing clouds of dust,
their faces wet with tears. No excuses,
just an emptiness about them.
Beyond worry. The journey over.
They open their mouths and sip
like sinners seeking redemption;
then enter the darkness that I am.
In this room without walls, they bolt
the door, lie down and wait for the cure
to wash it all away: white as the winter sky.
A shower of hair over a pillow, a last memory.

*The potion:*

*Seven days when no one calls.*
*Seven nights when nothing stirs.*
*Seven walks in the rain.*
*Seven ferocious prayers.*
*Seven gentle curses.*
*Seven lakes to swim in.*
*Seven woods to wander in.*
*Seven axes to cut away the wood.*
*Seven blades to cut away the skin.*

*Seven beds to toss in.*
*Seven master plans.*
*Seven panic attacks.*
*Seven circles of the asylum.*
*Seven hairs from the pillow.*
*Seven howls of rage.*
*Seven memories erased*
*Seven hours staring out the window.*
*Seven currachs ready for the voyage.*
*Seven bags of books.*
*Seven paintings.*
*Seven empty rooms.*
*Seven sleep filled nights*
*Seven songs of thanks.*

How to mix this cure,
where best to take it,
depends on who you are.
I wonder if everything's here –
at its terrible cost,
I'd hate to think anything's lost.

CURE FOR MELANCHOLIA

This is one of the easiest cures,
though it's potent only a short while,
and sadly is not strong enough
to work on poets or painters
whose subject is the female nude.

Women should take it
when the moon is full,
though I've heard the old say
it's best mixed in sunlight
or at least when there's
a break in the clouds.

First take a sprinkling
of river water from stretches
where the current is strong.
To this, add a few sloes,
a few blackberries,
one wild strawberry,
a little cinnamon. Next,

add a handful of grass
from an old hill fort
and a small bowl of nuts
from a hazel tree,
an orange
and a few raspberries –
for they are childhood.

To give the potion
a little lift,
add the blood of a swallow

and a feather from
its soft white breast.
Finally, squeeze in the juice

from three yellow lemons.
Then take a clean round pot –
nothing with tin or aluminium –
and pour in a bottle of red wine.
Now heat over an open flame.

When the liquid begins to move
mix in the lot and stir and breathe
and stir and breathe and stir...
strain, and drink before it cools.

Now sit by your fire
or better, lie in bed.

And if you share your life
with another weary soul,
stay off subjects such as
home improvements,
gardening,
children's education,
sexual satisfaction.

Stay in bed until
the weather changes,
take the cure
as often as necessary,
or until winter passes
your bit of sky.

CURE FOR LONELINESS

This is an old Russian cure,
better than a cup of tea,
more reliable than pills.
It was first formulated
by Leo Tolstoy in the
long winter of 1869.
A complex potion,
the recipe runs to 1,144 pages,
too long to put down here
but you'll find it on the creaking
shelves of any library
under the title *War and Peace*.

I suggest you take it
late at night,
beside an open fire,
with a map of Old Russia
and a bottle of red wine.
I tried it myself
and it worked fine on me:
all the ghosts in my head
gathered round to hear
the tale of love and loss.

You could also try
some very old remedies
by Homer or Catullus,
or powerful ones
by Dante or Shakespeare,
or witches' brews

by Sappho or Tsvetayeva,
or complex Irish potions
by Messrs Joyce and Beckett.
Their cures hold a mirror up
to your soul. They work
incredibly well. Though
I have found them addictive,
and the Beckett repeats
at odd times of the night.

These days
there is a whole
new range of panaceas:
heal-alls, cure-alls.
Some are like fire,
others like ice, but
none have been
tested by time.
However,
I do recommend,
for those darkest days,
the small healing potions
of Michael Hartnett.

New Poems: Tossing the Feathers
(2006)

# Foraging

And in the evening,
I seem always to answer
with the same reply:

I have been in the yard
making, cleaning and dancing –
tossing the feathers.

# The Dead Time of the Year

The way the day folds in on itself
as the dark of evening settles
over the hills and the exhausted fields –

you'd think there'd be more to it
than that, but I have been watching
this silent surrender for years

and the day's end is always the same.
We put it away with the other old memories
saying: *That wasn't so bad after all.*

When I was a child I could hear
God turning the cogs
as he put away the light.

I would say he slept
with it under his pillow
to keep the devil at bay.

My little dreams were full of footsteps,
all blind creatures
stumbling about in the dark –

never a night without them.
It is a wonder I slept at all
through the dead time of the year.

And here I am again, home.
The old place, mine now,
mine and the hours.

I stand watching as darkness touches
the rise and fall of all the spilt
world beyond my window.

I am stirred by her devotion
to the least of things:
forest, field, the broken gate.

Restless. Alone. A jealous man.
I leave the lamp unlit
and let her darkness take me too.

*That wasn't such a bad day after all.*

# Odd

"He's odd!" was how my grandmother
always introduced me to strangers:
odd women on the steps of churches,
odd men we'd meet on our way
to visit the dying, the bereaved,
someone who could tell her about the end.
She never brought flowers.
I can't even imagine
she brought much comfort,
just herself and myself.

She'd point at me and say, "He's odd!"
as if to explain my silence.
"There isn't one of them right.
It's from the father's side,
all priests and teetotal.
Not that there's anything wrong with that,
but it weakens the blood.
I have raised this lad myself,
all innocence and shiftiness.
You could write a book about him."
Then she would fall silent
as if imagining the pages fluttering.

I remember one evening
this dying woman asking
"How's he doing at school?"
"Terrible," my grandmother said,

"Terrible. Only this morning his teacher
said, 'He's very good at poetry.'
And you know what that means?"
"Yes," said the dying woman,
"he's like myself, useless at everything."

# The Sad Daughter's Tale

Except for the hair
and a dusting of white skin
the rest was pink
as if a fish
had been slit open
going over a stone
at a shallow
part of the river
close to the edge
amongst the reeds
in November or December.

Somewhere in the hills
a wildness
mountains high
forests dark,
flowers gone to seed.

There are no miracles here.
You can get lost in this land
learn a sad song
sing it your whole life long.

# Sheltering

God left four islands
off the coast where I live.
For the birds mostly,
herons, gannets.
Though in summer
there are a drizzle of sheep,
a few grey seals
and the odd, poor soul
who rows out to touch
these unsheltered,
forgotten bits of earth.

This I understand, as I too
am drawn to islands:
their rocky souls,
their little thatch of green –
that eternal stillness.

Though fishermen say,
in darkness islands lift
their seaweed dresses
and dance, or follow
a mile or two after sail,
so that in the morning
the night watch
tells the skipper
he saw whales.

I have never seen this.
I have watched the islands
from my window
persevere while all

around them is unsettled,
restless and moving.

These days
I feel the sadness
of John Donne's line:
"No man is an island."
We are nothing
as steadfast
or as glorious.
As our seas rise –
as the words
and the dishes
begin to fly –
we pack up
and run for shelter.

# The Master Weaver

*for* Barbara

Did I tell you about that time in Allihies,
after reading in the old schoolhouse,
I got talking to an elderly Englishwoman
dressed in tweed, quiet as a field,
with a smile that spoke of church fêtes,
privet hedges and cream teas.
Though that rug was quickly pulled
when she told me she'd lived in Paris
for fifty years and was a master weaver.
I saw her string words together like pearls.
When she asked which writers I admired,
I told her I loved Samuel Beckett.
"Ah yes," she said, "Sam. So did I.
His touch so warm, his eyes so blue."

# Beckettian Clerihews

Samuel Beckett
the man who said "feck it!
I'll kneel down but I'll not pray,
even if it is Judgment Day."

Vladimir and Estragon
have waited their whole life long,
but Godot is married now, content,
and has long forgotten the appointment.

Happy days,
unhappy nights –
I can't dream on,
I must dream on.

Footfalls
in the halls
and all through the house,
the lonely, lonely ghost of a mouse.

All that fall
the autumn's call:
the forest leaves,
the empty trees.

Endgame,
always the same.
Checkmate,
that's our fate.

# Self Portrait

*— after* Samuel Beckett

A long way after!

# The Knot

There is a photograph
of Robert Frost wearing
a grey crombie,
a black waistcoat
and a white shirt,
much like I do.

But unlike me,
he is wearing a tie.
Not a big silk tent
that a businessman
might wear, but
a piece of twisted leather,
something you might
hang a bell on, a strap
taken from a horse's harness.

As for the knot,
it is a higgle tied by a child:
something done
and done
and done
until the juice is wrung
from the tie and it looks
like a dried orange rind.

Then there's the face:
even in black and white,

though the pallor is grey,
the look is self-satisfied,
content. And he has not
come from the hills,
because, for once,
his hair is combed.

Looking at the photograph,
I'd like to imagine the picture
was taken the morning after
he published *North of Boston*
or wrote *Stopping by Woods
on a Snowy Evening.*

But then there are the eyes:
so full of black doubt.
I think the truth of it is
he has been reading
in colleges and town halls
for the past few months
and is lost: a poet grown
tired of his own voice
and the crowded road
that is taking him
miles from home.

# Seven Haiku for Sahoko's Drawing

*Stillness*

Here is my stillness
light as Japanese maple –
falling in autumn.

*Work*

I work in this field,
the woman you see helps me –
it's all in the hands.

*Fall*

Before last night's storm
earth was clothed in green leaf –
now all has fallen.

*Moon*

When I wear my skin
I pull it tight as a coat –
lie still as the moon.

*Snow*

You spoke of crossing,
of leaving before the snows –
there's no sign of you.


*Less*

Down to the whiteness
my hands, my feet hold on to
less and less and less.


*Autumn*

Dreamt in October,
this is Sahoko's drawing –
autumn unveiling.

# Dublin – The New Year

My friend Li Po tells me
in his country it is the Year
of the Snow Leopard,
whose sign is the burning paw.

Not knowing what it is here,
but looking up at all the new
buildings that are beating
the curves out of the old city,

I tell him, in Dublin
it is the Year of the Crane,
whose sign is the wooden
board, the yellow jacket.

Houses, apartments,
mews, lofts;
luxurious residential
developments –

these are the prayers on the lips
of every pilgrim in this city,
whose final word
is not '*Amen*' but '*Sold*'.

# Seventeen Bridges

Everywhere I go
I arrive at a bridge –
all roads lead to them.

~

The moon on the bridge,
yellow light on the water –
first night of winter.

~

Mid-way cross the bridge
I look into the river,
going with the flow

~

The Liffey's old song
singing softly below me
in a muddy voice.

~

Crossing the stone bridge
all of Dublin Bay unfolds –
the young city cranes.

~

Life is a small bridge
over the river of time –
careful on the ledge.

~

As she crossed the bridge
my grandmother read the sky,
searching for good news.

~

Seven bridges built
in Dublin last year, seven
homes for the homeless.

~

Sometimes when I look
into the eyes of bridges,
I see my lost soul.

~

You say that our hurt
is water under the bridge,
troubles washed away.

~

The bridge and the tree
sleeping on the still water:
natural affection.

~

Mother on one bank
father on the other side;
I'm still in between.

~

Over and done with
now you've burnt all your bridges –
ashes in the wind.

~

Water will tickle
the green legs of old bridges
willing them to dance.

~

Cars and clouds above,
boats and fishes below –
the bridge's old boast.

~

The end of the day,
as I cross the bridge to home
the river flows on.

~

Philosophers say
no matter how strong the bridge,
water is stronger

# The Poet and the Mouse

I killed the shy brown mouse
that came to winter in my house.

This quiet, natural part of God's plan
was set upon by Man.

I placed the trap upon the floor,
waited behind the kitchen door.

I buried her in the garden
beneath the leaves and tumble down.

Where was the good in what I had done
when all she wanted was a few stale crumbs?

What ailed me to want to kill
the little creature from the hill?

Grey the hour, grey the day
I went and took a life away.

## Six Twenty-five a.m.

I notice the birds go to church
more often than the people now;
they roost on the roof and sing.
I wonder what God makes of
their feathers and their twittering?
Of course the birds are
more primitive than us,
they were singing
before the crosses came
and they will sing
when the crosses are gone.

I have seen them
in the ruins of monasteries
come down from the trees
to sing among the stones.
And in graveyards, they have
no fear of shadow or ghost,
for they make their nests
in the yew trees beside the graves
and sing, and sing, and sing
as if the poor souls lying there
should be happy.

# The Well in the Rain

*i.m.* Kevin Curtis 1921-2004

I

AND WHEN THE HEART

*One fine morning when my life is over*
*I'll fly away, O Lordy, I'll fly away...*

and when the heart gives out
when the breath
and the beating are gone

when the bones heave up
on their final shore
when the voice is still for evermore

when the room is so quiet
you can hear death
beginning its old sad song –

the eternal lament of the heart's last beat.

~

That's the thing about the weather –
every day in Ireland
is a good day for a funeral
unless you're burying your own father
then it's a horse of a day.

~

Sometimes I lie in bed at night
wondering about the dead.
Asleep, but wondering:

*Do you think they're gone to a land of song,*
*do you think they're gone and they belong?*

*Do you think they're gone to the forest deep,*
*do you think they're gone and their fears all sleep?*

*Do you think they're gone where the clouds all go,*
*do you think they're gone with an easy flow?*

*Do you think they're gone where the prayers are true,*
*do you think they pray for me and you?*

*Do you think they're gone where the winds all blow,*
*do you think they walk through a land of snow?*

*Do you think they're gone to the river's end,*
*do you think they're gone and they've found a friend?*

*Do you think they're gone where the stars go out,*
*do you think they're gone or are they still about?*

All his life my father
made and mended things:
bicycles to begin with,
then motor bikes,
tabernacles for churches,

small chalices
that held the body
and blood of Christ.

Between buying
his first Ford Prefect
and his first Ford Anglia,
he made my first wardrobe.
Sad to say,
I blew it up
one summer making
blackberry wine.

He was always
scraping and papering.
He wore a brown coat
covered in paint and glue.
Some days he would
shimmy from his shed
covered in dust
looking like Michelangelo.

He would have been
making something
for my mother,
a new rail for the stairs,
a green box to hold
the Christmas tree.
Now her forest is felled,
the wood is silent,

the season turns
from autumn to winter.
I'll remember him there
in the corner, making.
As he grew old
his hands were always cold.
Still, he like a job done right;
the story well told.

Even as he lay dying
he was measuring the clouds
above bed twenty-three
in St. Patrick's Ward.
Until, finally, with his
last few breaths,
he lifted his arms and
began painting heaven's door,

making it ready for us
who'll follow after.

II

HYMN TO LIFE

The humpity sand dunes
on the edge of the beach
is where I go for quiet.

Not that there is
much of that to be found,
not with the waves sighing.

Not that I mind.
Over the years I've
gotten used to the tears.

The gulls are the worst,
crying all hours of the day.
At night it's the sea that moans.

I hate to say it, but sometimes
I join in; long, deep sighs
coming over the dunes,

with the waves, the wind and the gulls
we're not exactly the Hallelujah Chorus,
more the *What-the-fuck-will-we-do-now Lament*.

# Close

The last entry in my father's journal
says that he has been mending pipes
but has grown a little tired, and so
he will begin again in the morning.

He never did. Death reached
down and stole his heart away.

And yet, though I've seen
that Thief up close:
felt His breath on my face;
His eyes on my soul,

I still believe that if I stop writing now,
and go out for coffee,
I can come back in an hour or two
and take up where I left off.

# Anniversary

*i.m* Michael Hartnett

Above the house
the wind is in the trees
and the river is in flood.

Left off the latch,
the out-house door
is swinging off its hinges.

That time of the year again
when the earth is restless
and the yellow moon is full.

If any ghost comes tonight
I'm sure it will be Michael,
dead four years this very eve.

I have lit a candle for him
but it went out hours ago.
So I sit here in the dark, listening

to the out-house door
swinging off its hinges.
I could go out and close it,

but who would wait for Michael?

# Coming Home After Watching Dancers

Coming home
    after watching dancers
and left wondering
    why nothing in me moves.
I am not the leaf, the river,
    the path or the cloud –
I am the tree,
    unmoving, rooted.
Past fifty,
    I usually blame the age in me.

But old Tom
    he's seventy-four
and his feet
    don't hardly touch the floor.
And Eileen,
    big and round as a pond,
her two red shoes
    are light as autumn leaves
and grace the wood.

But me,
    I hardly kick the dust,
or worry
    the tune.
I fade into the corner
    and wonder
why nothing in me moves.

Half past three,
    the road home,
the music

        is in the trees now –
the stars take up
        where the dancers left off:
they shine in the dark,
        they shine in the dark.

# The Family Tree

His mother told me he was
conceived under an apple tree
and it was this that gave him
his great way with horses –
she said they could smell
the apples on his skin.

True, he had green eyes
and a leafy look,
and he told me that once
when he was lost in a forest
they used a horse to find him, a small
child with apple blossom in his hair.

He married a girl from
the north country. He always
spoke of her mane of curls.
Dead now. He buried her
out on the hills; every autumn
she is covered in leaves.

A fruitful man,
he had seven daughters.
He kept them round him
like an orchard.
Their dappled light attracted
farmers, foresters, fools with no land,

boys with green sap
still rising in their skin.
He watched them
as they swayed

and when the season turned,
they blossomed – greens and reds

and yellows, flower and leaf.
You should have heard the birds singing;
the bees, the butterflies,
even the river seemed to gurgle.
The woods were all fern and wild herbs
until the autumn – the leaving and the dying.

He was known to grow sullen in winter
mumbling about moss and wood rot,
saying he could feel the loss
of every leaf as if it was a wound.
I saw him last week down by the river,
birds singing on his outstretched arms.

He was older, looking more than ever
like an ancient apple tree.
I crossed the field to stand in his shade.
And this is as far as my poem can go –
the family tree reaches into the future.
So much depends on what happens next:

storm or gale, frost or ice.
Depends on how long he can stand there
watching the meadow greening;
the horses moving in his shadow;
the leaves falling like lost children,
again, and again, and again.

# Biographical note

TONY CURTIS was born in Dublin in 1955. He is the author
of six warmly received collections of poetry, the most recent of
which – *What Darkness Covers* – was published by Arc in 2003.
In that year also he was the recipient of the Varuna House
Exchange Fellowship to Australia.

Curtis has been awarded the Irish National Poetry Prize
and is a member of Aosdána, the Irish academy of the arts.